LEGENDS OF WARFARE
GROUND

Stuart Tank, Vol. 2
The M5, M5A1, and Howitzer Motor Carriage M8 Versions in World War II

DAVID DOYLE

SCHIFFER MILITARY

4880 Lower Valley Road   Atglen, PA 19310

Designed by Justin Watkinson
Type set in Impact/Minion Pro/Univers LT Std

ISBN: 978-0-7643-5823-4
Printed in China

Published by Schiffer Publishing, Ltd.
4880 Lower Valley Road
Atglen, PA 19310
Phone: (610) 593-1777; Fax: (610) 593-2002
E-mail: Info@schifferbooks.com
www.schifferbooks.com

For our complete selection of fine books on this and related subjects, please visit our website at www.schifferbooks.com.
You may also write for a free catalog.

Schiffer Publishing's titles are available at special discounts for bulk purchases for sales promotions or premiums. Special editions, including personalized covers, corporate imprints, and excerpts, can be created in large quantities for special needs. For more information, contact the publisher.

We are always looking for people to write books on new and related subjects. If you have an idea for a book, please contact us at proposals@schifferbooks.com.

Acknowledgments

As with all of my projects, this book would not have been possible without the generous help of many friends. Instrumental to the completion of this book were Tom Kailbourn, Rob Ervin, 14th Armored Re-Creations, Brent Mullins, Scott Taylor, Kurt Laughlin, Jim Gilmore, Joe Demarco, the staff and volunteers at the Patton Museum, and the staff at the National Archives. Most importantly, I am blessed to have the help and support of my wife, Denise, for which I am eternally grateful.

All photos are from the collection of the US National Archives and Records Administration, unless otherwise noted.

Contents

Introduction

While the M3 family of vehicles had won respect for their reliability after their initial combat showing in North Africa, the vehicles still had some weaknesses. For one, the 37 mm main gun, thought by many to be wildly inadequate in the European theater, would plague the Stuart throughout its production. The other major weakness was its reliance on an air-cooled radial engine, the W-670, which was in considerable demand due to its use in Stearman PT-17 training aircraft. In June 1941, the Ordnance Department began aggressive efforts to reengine the light tank, and the result was the M5, the subject of this volume.

Although, owing to its 37 mm gun, the M5 and its successor the M5A1 were obsolete for European tank versus tank duels even as the vehicles rolled off the Cadillac assembly lines, the tank was still vastly superior to a rifle-armed infantryman. Although replaced on the production lines by the M24 during the war, the tanks nevertheless soldiered on through the end of the conflict and in postwar years served in the armies of many allied nations.

Today the tanks are prized by collectors, in large part due to their compact size, which means that they can be trucked over the road without the need for overwidth or overweight permits.

Specifications			
MODEL	**M5**	**M5A1**	**M8**
Weight*	33,100 lbs.	34,700 lbs.	34,600 lbs.
Length	174.8 in.	190.5 in.	196 in.
Width	88.3 in.	90 in.	91.5 in.
Height	102 in.	101 in.	107 in.
Tread	88.3 in.	73.3 in.	73.5 in.
Crew	4	4	4
Maximum speed	36 mph	36 mph	36 mph
Fuel capacity	89 gals.	89 gals.	89 gals.
Range	100 miles	100 miles	100 miles
Electrical	12-volt negative ground	12-volt negative ground	12-volt negative ground
Transmission Speeds	4 Forward/1 Reverse	4 Forward/1 Reverse	4 Forward/1 Reverse
Turning radius	42 ft.	42 ft.	42 ft.
Armament			
Main	37 mm	37 mm	37 mm
Secondary	2 x .30-cal.	2 x .30-cal.	2 x .30-cal.
Flexible	1 x .30-cal.	75 mm	1 x .50-cal.
Engine Data			
Engine make/model	Cadillac Series 42		
Number of cylinders	16 (8 per engine)		
Cubic-inch displacement	692		
Horsepower	296		
Torque	560		
Radio Equipment			

M5 and M5A1 vehicles were equipped either with SCR-508, SCR-528, or SCR-538, all with integral interphones. Again, the SCR-506 was fitted to command tanks.

M8 Howitzer Motor Carriages had the SCR-510 radio set and the RC-99 interphone set.

M3A3 vehicles were equipped with either SCR-508, -528, or -538 radios, all with integral interphones. Again, the SCR-506 was fitted to command tanks.

* Fighting weight.

The first three generations of the Stuart Light Tank, the M3, the M3A1 (shown here), and the M3A3, were all powered by the air-cooled radial engines. Nimble and having notable simplicity and reliability, the British dubbed the tanks "Honey"—but there was still room for improvement.

The final production version of the Stuart with an air-cooled engine was the M3A3, which had a much-improved ballistic shape as well as an improved, enlarged turret. The M3A3 used a air-cooled Continental W-670 radial engine. These engines were similar to radial aircraft engines, and production of the type strained an already overburdened capacity for producing such power plants.

CHAPTER 1
Light Tank M5

As the war progressed, the increased demand for radial engines both for tank and airplane production forced the Ordnance Department to search for alternative power plants. By June 1941, they had come upon the novel idea of installing two V-8 gasoline Cadillac automobile engines into the Light Tank M3. The installation featured two automatic transmissions and an automatic auxiliary transmission in the front of the driver. This combination was found to provide both sound power and reliability.

An alternative hull design was required to house the new power train. The pilot model was initially named Light Tank M4, but by the time production began, the Medium Tank M4 was also in production. As a result, it was renamed Light Tank M5.

The turret from the Light Tank M3A1 was used and remained nearly unchanged. The sloped frontal armor of the new hull was similar to the M3A3, but the hull side armor was vertical. Also like the M3A3, the driver and assistant driver were provided with hatches in the forward hull roof. A few initial production tanks were equipped with a fixed machine gun in the glacis armor, but they lacked a ventilator fan between the hull hatches.

As a testament to their design, the suspension components of the M3 series were retained, although the weight of the vehicle had increased by nearly 4,000 pounds.

General Motors and Massey-Harris produced a total of 2,074 tanks by December 1942, and they first saw action during Operation Torch in North Africa.

In 1941, the radial engines that were being used in the Light Tank M3 were increasingly in demand in the Army. Thus, during that year the experimental Light Tank M3E2 was created. It was a modification of Light Tank M3, serial number 752, with two Cadillac 1G-series V-8 automobile engines with Hydramatic transmissions and an auxiliary automatic transmission replacing the Continental W-670-9A radial engines and the Synchromesh standard transmission. After the M3E2 performed well in tests, the vehicle was again modified, with a new, homogeneous steel upper hull and D58101 turret, in which guise it was designated M3E3, as seen here. The M3E3 served as the pilot for the Light Tank M5. *General Motors LLC*

The M3E3 was assigned Army registration number W-303748, and that number is visible toward the rear of the sponson. In most respects, the shape of the Light Tank M3E3 would carry over to the production Light Tank M5. *General Motors LLC*

The left side of the Light Tank
M3E3 is in view. The engine deck
had a prominent "hump" toward
the rear; this was in large part to
provide room for the radiators,
which were positioned above the
twin Cadillac engines. *General
Motors LLC*

The M3E3 is viewed from above,
showing the design of the glacis,
the new driver's and assistant
driver's hatch doors and their
substantial hinges, the turret roof,
and the engine deck. Ventilation
grilles of expanded-steel mesh
were located on the front and the
top rear of the hump over the
engine compartment. A fixed
.30-caliber machine gun, fired by
the driver, was located at the
center of the glacis; there also was
a .30-caliber machine gun on the
right side of the glacis. The purpose
of the arch-shaped frame on the
front right corner of the glacis is
not clear. *General Motors LLC*

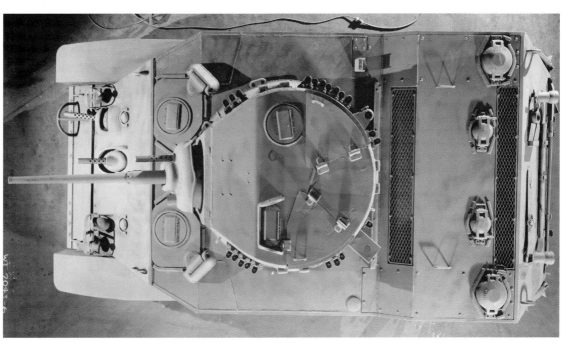

A Cadillac Series 42 V-8 water-cooled engine and Hydramatic transmission of the type used on the M3E3 and subsequently on the Light Tanks M5 and M5A1 is displayed. Two such engines were installed in each vehicle. Each engine had a displacement of 346 cubic inches. The engine exhausts were routed downward to the muffler. *General Motors LLC*

The Light Tank M5, of which the M3E3 was the prototype, was produced in its entirety during 1942. The Cadillac Motor Car Division of General Motors, Detroit; the Southern California Division of GM, South Gate, California; and Massey-Harris, Racine, Wisconsin, completed 2,074 M5s, with production ending in December 1942. *General Motors LLC*

A Light Tank M5 with the hatches buttoned up is driving up an incline at a desert training or testing center. The suspension and running gear of the M5 remained from the Light Tank M3 and M3A1. The placement of the radio antenna on the front left portion of the engine deck was a typical one. The turret for the M5 was the D58101. *General Motors LLC*

The rear of the hull of Light Tank M5 serial number 1, is portrayed in a photo taken on April 30, 1942. The engine-access doors are open; these were of bifolding design. Inside the round openings in the bulkhead inside the doors are the two Cadillac 1G-series V-8 automobile engines and their cooling fans. The engine exhausts exit the lower part of the bulkhead; the right exhaust is partially hidden by the right doors. On the overhang of the rear of the upper hull at the top of the photo are pioneer tools. *General Motors LLC*

ASSEMBLY LINE
M5A1 Light Tank

The Summary Report of Tank-Automotive Material Acceptances lists a total of 6,810 M5A1 light tanks as having been produced by three firms. Those were Cadillac, in Detroit and Southgate, American Car and Foundry, and Massey-Harris. This is the Massey-Harris production line, where 1,084 M5A1s were built.

The rear of the hull of Light Tank M5 serial number 1, is portrayed in a photo taken on April 30, 1942. The engine-access doors are open; these were of bifolding design. Inside the round openings in the bulkhead inside the doors are the two Cadillac 1G-series V-8 automobile engines and their cooling fans. The engine exhausts exit the lower part of the bulkhead; the right exhaust is partially hidden by the right doors. On the overhang of the rear of the upper hull at the top of the photo are pioneer tools. *General Motors LLC*

CHAPTER 2
Light Tank M5A1

Because of the development of the M3A3, a similar turret was developed for the M5 Light Tank. It also had a bustle at the rear, and it could mount either the SCR-508 radio or the British No. 19 radio set.

The result of the combination of this turret with the M5 hull was standardized as the Light Tank M5A1. The side armor of the turret was initially equipped with pistol ports, but these were quickly eliminated. They are often seen welded up on early-production tanks. Also as in the M3A3, larger hatches facilitated turret egress in an emergency. The antiaircraft machine gun mount now occupied the right side of the turret, rather than the rear. A sloping armored shield that stored a swiveling mount for the .30-caliber machine gun was a feature of later production models.

General Motors, American Car and Foundry, and Massey-Harris produced the M5A1. It began to replace the M5 in production in November 1942, and a total of 6,810 were manufactured before production ceased in June 1944. This made it the most numerous US light tank of the war. Of that total, over 1,500 were provided to Commonwealth armies through the Lend-Lease Act.

New components continued to be introduced during production. Later models featured solid stamped road wheel faces, attached sand shields, a rear-mounted stowage bin on the lower hull, and a sloping armored shield on the right side of the turret.

Although undergunned and underarmored by the time of its introduction, the M5A1 served until the end of the war both in Europe and the Pacific.

The Light Tank M5A1 mated the hull of the Light Tank M5 with a turret similar to the one used on the M3A3. This combination yielded the benefits of the new hull and drive train of the M5 with a turret capable of holding in its bustle the requisite radio sets of either the US Army or the British and Commonwealth armies. A total of 6,810 M5A1s were produced between November 1942 and June 1944, by three corporations: Cadillac, Detroit; Southern California Division of GM, South Gate; Massey-Harris, Racine, Wisconsin; and American Car and Foundry, Berwick, Pennsylvania. Seen here is Cadillac-built M5A1, serial number 1182, at Aberdeen Proving Ground, in Maryland, on December 1, 1942.

The nickname "CREIGHTON" is marked in small letters on the sponson of this Light Tank M5A1. A registration number is present on the sponson but is too faint to positively discern. While some M5A1s were delivered with open-spoke bogie wheels, this example has solid-disk wheels. The antiaircraft mount was at the center of the right side of the turret. Also on the side of the turret are grousers.

The roof of the turret of Light Tank M5A1 serial number 2145, photographed by the Ordnance Operation, General Motors Proving Ground, on February 13, 1943, was nearly identical to the turret roof of the Light Tank M3A3 portrayed earlier in volume 1. Also in view are details of the upper part of the hull, including hold-down straps and armored filler covers on the engine deck. The large, outboard fillers were for fuel, while the smaller, inboard fillers were for coolant.

A newly minted, Cadillac-built Light Tank M5A1 is observed from the front left. Whereas the prominent splash guard, also called deflector, on the glacis of the Light Tank M3A3 was continuous, with an angled jog to the lower left of the bow machine gun, there were two separate splash guards on the glacis of the M5A1, the right-hand one being shorter and lower than the one on the left.

ASSEMBLY LINE

M5A1 Light Tank

The Summary Report of Tank-Automotive Material Acceptances lists a total of 6,810 M5A1 light tanks as having been produced by three firms. Those were Cadillac, in Detroit and Southgate, American Car and Foundry, and Massey-Harris. This is the Massey-Harris production line, where 1,084 M5A1s were built.

Various preserved and operational Light Tanks M5A1 are portrayed in the following series of color photographs. This example, hull draped in camouflage netting, is equipped with a mix of bogie wheel types. Three are the stamped-metal wheels with rubber tires that were produced starting in 1943 by the Kelsey-Hayes Wheel Company. The next-to-last wheel is the earlier, five-spoked variety with steel plugs welded over the holes between the spokes.

The same vehicle, operated by 14th Armored Re-Creations, is seen in action. On the side of the turret is the armored shield for the exterior .30-caliber machine gun. When the gun was not in use, it could be swung down into the shield for protection during travel. *Photo by author*

This M5A1 has all Kelsey-Hayes bogie wheels on the left side. Protruding from the left front of the 37 mm gun shield is a long sun shield. Grousers stored on the side of the turret added an added degree of protection from projectiles. *Photo by author*

On the rear of the hull is a storage box made of sheet metal, with a hinged top and a storage bin on its rear. The bin has a metal frame and sides and expanded-steel mesh on the bottom and rear. This box-and-bin combination was a feature on late-production M5A1s. *Photo by author*

The same M5A1 portrayed in the preceding photo is viewed from another perspective. The gunner and the vehicle commander have separate hatch doors in the roof of the turret, but when both hatches are open, they appear to be one large hatch door. *Photo by author*

Several M5A1s are rolling across a field during a reenactment. The closest vehicle bears registration number 3049409, which pertains to an April 1944, Cadillac-built M5A1. Cadillac ceased production of the M5A1 the following month. *Photo by author*

The crew of this M5A1 have applied mud camouflage over the Olive Drab base color. A good view is available of the positioning of the pioneer tools stored on the rear of the upper hull. An air deflector is under the overhang of the rear of the upper hull, and an exhaust deflector is at the bottom rear of the lower hull. Both deflectors were equipped with grilles on late-production M5A1s, and those grilles are visible here. The grille over the exhaust deflector is interrupted by a tow pintle, another late-production feature. *Photo by author*

This M5A1, owned and restored by Brent Mullins, is equipped with a detachable windshield for the driver, used in conjunction with a canvas foul-weather hood that was placed over the hatch to keep out the elements. The windshield was supplied with a wiper, and the unit is seen here stored on brackets affixed to the glacis. On the inside of the driver's hatch door is a periscope on a rotating base.
Photo by author

This M5A1 lacks the shield for the exterior .30-caliber machine gun. Before the gun shields with the gun mounts that pivoted down for storing the gun were introduced on late-production M5A1s, the gun mount was a nonfolding pedestal that was screwed to the side of the turret. *Photo by author*

A late-production M5A1 is viewed from the front. The detachable windshield for the driver is in a partially raised position. Below the windshield, and also just above the bow machine-gun ball mount, are two peephole plugs with U-shaped splash guards. *Mike Koening*

A rear view of a late-production Light Tank M5A1 shows the rears of the turret and hull. The radio antenna is mounted on a base attached to a removable panel on the rear of the turret bustle. This panel was removed when it was necessary to pull the 37 mm gun from the turret or to remount it. Also in view are the grilles for the air and exhaust deflectors on the rear of the lower hull. *Mike Koening*

The assistant driver's hatch door is viewed close-up. The Periscope M6 on the rotating mount on the door is installed, causing the sprung lid to rise up. A splash guard is welded to the hull roof on the outboard side of the hatch. On the inboard side of the hatch is the armored hood for the ventilator for the driver and assistant driver. *Photo by author*

The driver's hatch door, the splash guard to its left side, and the brackets for the windshield are shown. The periscopes were protected by brush guards fastened with hex nuts to the rotating base. *Photo by author*

The assistant driver's hatch door is open, revealing the inner side of the rotating periscope mount and the installed periscope, as well as the grab handle. Also in view are the gun shield, coaxial .30-caliber machine gun barrel, and details of the frontal plate of the turret, on which foundry marks are visible. Note the open bottom on the shield for the antiaircraft machine gun behind the open hatch door. *Photo by author*

A driver's windshield, complete with windshield wiper and motor, is stored on its brackets. The windshield is secured by a latch on each side; these latches, when attached to the lugs at the tops of the brackets, also served to hold the windshield in the "up" position. *Photo by author*

The driver's compartment is viewed through the open hatch. Just inside the hatch at the top are steering and braking controls and, dimly visible, the instrument panel. On the floor to the front of the seat is the accelerator pedal. To the right is the transfer unit, and to the left above the floor is a stored Periscope M6. *Mike Koening*

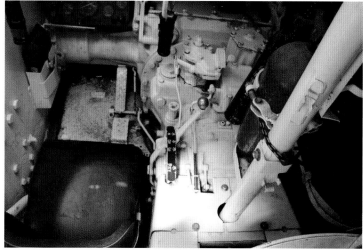

The transfer unit, next to the driver's seat, receives power, through the drive shafts, from the two engines and transmissions in the rear of the vehicle and transmits that power to the final-drive assembly. The lever with the brass knob to the right of the seat is the gear selector. *Photo by author*

In a view of the driver's compartment from below the turret, on the left side are the brake and steering controls (mounted on the ceiling), the dark-colored plug and retainer chain for the driver's peephole (on the glacis), the instrument panel, the left side of the final-drive assembly and the transfer unit, and, above the transfer unit, a headlight assembly stored on a bracket. Toward the upper right is the ventilator. *Photo by author*

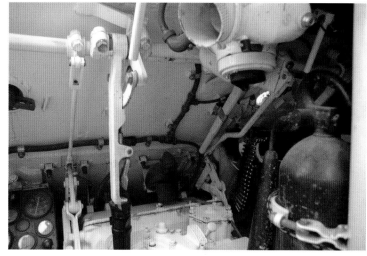

The driver's right steering and braking lever and its linkages, the ventilator, a red fire extinguisher, and the stored headlight are viewed from the driver's perspective. *Photo by author*

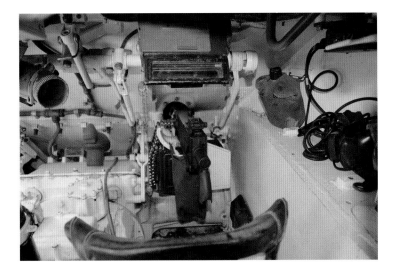

The assistant driver's compartment, as viewed from behind the seat, includes an M6 Periscope (*top*), steering and braking controls, and the .30-caliber bow machine gun and ammunition box. At the top left is the ventilator duct for the assistant driver. *Photo by author*

The assistant driver's compartment is viewed through the hatch. At the bottom is the cross-shaft of the braking and steering controls. Both seats are mounted on apparatuses that raise and lower them. Part of the mechanism is visible between the seat and the side of the lower hull. *Mike Koening*

The assistant driver's compartment is viewed from a different perspective. Above the machine gun on the glacis, the peephole plug has been removed, allowing light to shine through. *Photo by author*

The left sprocket assembly and the front bogie assembly are shown. These are the thirteen-toothed model, Ordnance number D59888, and are screwed to the hub, Ordnance number D59888. Also found on M5s and M5A1s were the D27468 sprockets; these had fourteen teeth and a scalloped inner perimeter. The bogie wheels are the stamped type by Kelsey-Hayes. To the upper rear of the bogie assembly is a track-support roller. *Mike Koening*

The track-support rollers (also called track-return rollers) were fitted with rubber tires. Locking wires are looped through the six hex screws holding the roller on its spindle. *Photo by author*

A bogie bracket is viewed from the rear, showing the two vertical volute springs housed within the unit. The design of these tapered springs allowed for liberal movement of the suspension arms. To the lower right is a close view of the rubber tire on a bogie wheel. *Photo by author*

The right-rear bogie assembly and the right idler assembly are the subject of this photo. Welded to the hull to the rear of the bogie wheel to the right is a lifting and tie-down hook, with two prongs arranged one over the other. *Photo by author*

This idler wheel is a late type, with a rubber tire, and steel plugs tack-welded over the teardrop-shaped openings between the spokes. The wheel is mounted on a fork-shaped suspension arm, the front end of which bears on a volute spring inside the idler bracket: a steel housing that is fastened to the hull. *Photo by author*

The box assembly, Ordnance number D60359, was a feature of late-production M5A1s. It was made of sheet metal and expanded-steel mesh and consisted of a sheet-metal box on the front and a bin for bedrolls and tarpaulins on the rear, with a hinged lid over the entire assembly. The mesh on the bin on the rear was designed to allow damp tarpaulins and bedrolls to air out. *Photo by author*

This idler wheel on an M5A1 has the teardrop-shaped openings between the spokes. Toward the rear of the suspension arm in view is the mechanism for adjusting track tension, by moving the idler wheel forward or aft. To accomplish this, the large hex nut in line with the axle of the wheel was loosened, and the nut on the threaded shaft was turned to move the wheel as desired. *Photo by author*

As seen on the right side of the storage box, the assembly was furnished with a hinged grab handle on each side, and there were three latches for the lid: one on the rear and one on each side. To the right of the box are the right taillight assembly and an armored box for a telephone handset. *Photo by author*

The engine deck of an M5A1 is viewed from the left side. Toward the left is a steel bar that was designed to prevent the 37 mm gun from being depressed sufficiently to shoot the storage box on the rear of the hull. The sloping rods in the right foreground and on the opposite side of the deck worked in conjunction with the main deflector bar. *Mike Koening*

Observed from the left side of the tank is the front ventilator grille for the engine-cooling system, with the rear of the turret and the bottom of the bustle to the upper left. The radiators are under the hump in the engine deck to the left. *Mike Koening*

An automatic towing pintle is mounted on the center bottom of the hull; these units were installed at the factories on M5A1s with serial numbers 5126 to 6500, 10170 to 10267, and 10369 and up. Details of the air deflector (*top*), the four-panel, bifolding doors for the engine compartment, and the exhaust deflector (*bottom*) also are in view. *Photo by author*

Light Tank M5A1, registration number 3048300, owned by the Veteran's Memorial Museum, Huntsville, Alabama, operates under the nickname "BAMA BELLE." The "S" following the registration number indicates a vehicle that has been equipped with radio-interference-suppression shielding.
Photo by author

The gun shield, frequently called the mantlet, is the M44 model, with the 37 mm gun barrel at the center, the aperture for the gunner's telescopic sight on the upper left side (facing forward), and the coaxial .30-caliber machine gun on the right side. A dented sun shield is over the sight aperture. Lifting eyes are welded to the upper front sides of the turret. *Photo by author*

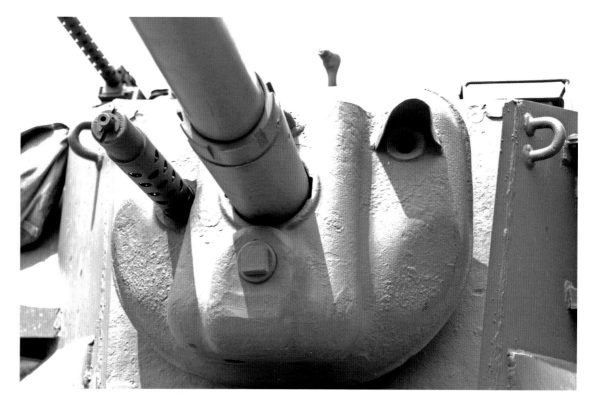

A Browning .30-caliber machine gun is on the external mount on the right side of the turret. This is the late-type mount with armored shield; the bottom of the mount pivoted so that the entire mount and gun could be swung down within the armored shield when not in use. On the rear of the mount is an A-frame travel lock for the machine gun. *Photo by author*

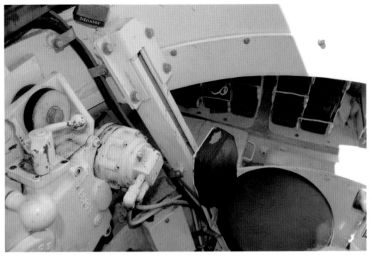

As seen from the left side of an M5A1 turret, the hatch doors are open, allowing a glimpse of the radio in the turret bustle. On the right (commander's) hatch door is a Periscope M6 on a rotating mount. Cushions, fixed grab handles, and pivoting handles are affixed to the interiors of the doors. On the opposite side of the turret, the machine gun mount is swung down to the stored position. On the front of the turret roof is a spotlight and two periscopes with brush guards. *Photo by author*

The turret of the M5A1 was traversed by means of the traversing gearbox at the lower left, between the commander's and gunner's seats. Normally the gearbox was powered hydraulically, but there was a hand crank on the gearbox (extreme lower left of the photo) by which the turret could be traversed manually in a pinch. The lever with the round knob on the top of the gearbox was the clutch control. To the lower right is the gunner's seat, mounted on a stanchion and height adjustable. In the background are storage racks for .30-caliber machine gun ammunition. *Photo by author*

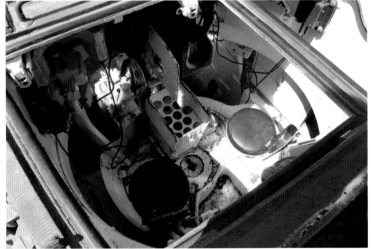

Radio sets that were installed in the M5A1 included the SCR-506 (command tanks only), SCR-508, SCR-528, or SCR-538. This set is an SCR-508, with a Radio Receiver BC-603 present on the right side of the photo. Above the radio equipment is its canvas cover. *Photo by author*

As seen through the open left hatch of an M5A1 turret, at the top center is the breech and guard of the 37 mm gun. A spent-casing deflector normally on the gun mount to the rear of the breech is missing. Below the gun are the gunner's and commander's seats and a rack for ready rounds of 37 mm ammunition. To the upper left is the cushioned headrest for the gunner's periscope. The gray box below the headrest is the power traverse control; the two paddle-shaped objects on the top of the control are triggers for the 37 mm and coaxial guns. *Mike Koening*

Again through the open left hatch, the eye guard for the gunner's Telescopic Sight M54 is to the lower left, to the right side of which are the recoil guard and the breech of the 37 mm gun. Below the telescopic sight and the gun breech are the elevating hand wheel for the Combination Gun Mount M44 and the ready-ammunition box for 37 mm rounds. To the right is the commander's seat. *Photo by author*

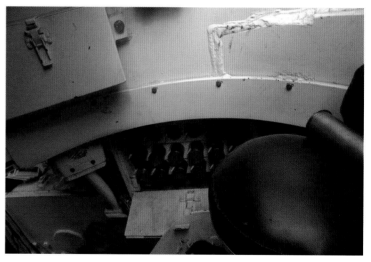

At the center is the 37 mm gun breech and operating handle. The Olive Drab object to the far right is the gyro control box, part of the gyrostabilizer, which acted to maintain the aim of the gun, in elevation, even while the vehicle was moving. Between the gyro control box and the 37 mm gun, the rear of the coaxial .30-caliber machine gun is visible. A tanker's helmet is propped up to the left side of the 37 mm gun. *Photo by author*

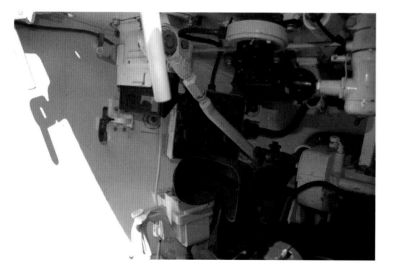

As seen from the upper rear of the 37 mm gun breech (*bottom right*), at the upper center are the gunner's periscope and the white link rod that moves the periscope in unison with the elevation of the gun. On the turret wall beyond the gunner's Telescopic Sight M54 is a switch box that includes the gyro switch and master switch. Below that box, the white-colored mechanism is the traverse control. To the upper right is the handle for controlling the spotlight from inside the turret. *Photo by author*

As seen from the left side of the turret, with the commander's seat to the right holding a 37 mm round, the 37 mm ammunition rack in the right sponson is in view. It is equipped with a bifolding door, which is in the open position, showing several brass casings inside. *Photo by author*

CHAPTER 3
Howitzer Motor Carriage M8

In keeping with the practice of having multiple uses for its tank chassis, development began in June of 1941 on mounting both 75 mm and 105 mm howitzers on the chassis of the M3. These experiments resulted in the pilot model T18 in early 1942, which featured a 75 mm howitzer within a fixed casemate. The limited traverse in this configuration was less than satisfactory, so work began on an open turret mount for the howitzer. Marrying that turret to the new Light Tank M5 resulted in pilot model T47, which was subsequently standardized as the M8 Howitzer Motor Carriage.

The majority of production used the M3 howitzer in mount M7. This was built with a cast gun mantlet 1½ inches thick and turret side armor 1 inch thick. A ring for a .50-caliber Browning machine gun was mounted in the turret roof. Racks for carrying track grousers were fitted on the external turret walls.

The power train of the M8 was identical to that of the Light Tank M5A1 with its Cadillac V-8 gasoline engines and automatic transmissions. The hull top hatches for the driver and assistant driver were eliminated due to the much-larger turret ring. The bow machine gun was also eliminated and the glacis armor was modified with two hatches in front of the drivers. While these forward hatches were closed, revolving top-mounted M9 periscopes provided all-around vision for the drivers.

Cadillac Motor Division began manufacture in September 1942, and a total of 1,778 vehicles were produced by January 1944. The M8 HMC was allocated to cavalry reconnaissance units and was used both by US and Free French forces in World War II.

The 75 mm Howitzer Motor Carriage (HMC) M8 mated the 75 mm Howitzer M3 on the Mount M7 in an open turret with the Light Tank M5A1 chassis, to produce a highly mobile, self-propelled light artillery piece for the close support of infantry and cavalry reconnaissance units. The Cadillac Division of General Motors produced the 75 mm HMC M8 from September 1942 to January 1944, completing a total of 1,778. Shown in these photos is the pilot M8 vehicle, registration number W-4051234, during trials at Aberdeen Proving Ground, Maryland, on September 22, 1942.

The 75 mm HMC M8 often was fitted with the T36E6 tracks, as seen here. These were double-pin, rubber-bushed, steel tracks with three parallel grousers on each track link, for improved traction. A basket with expanded-steel mesh construction was on the rear of the turret, for storing a folded tarpaulin. On the upper rear of the turret was a mount for a .50-caliber machine gun for antiaircraft defense.

The 75 mm howitzer and the .50-caliber machine gun both are at maximum elevation in this left-side view of 75 mm HMC M8 pilot A1 and registration number W-4051234. Note the vertical weld bead on the side of the turret to the front of the lifting eye.

As seen in an elevated view of 75 mm HMC M8 pilot A1 at Aberdeen on September 22, 1942, the .50-caliber machine gun was installed on a ring mount on the left rear of the turret. The gunner sat on the round seat to the right of the 75 mm howitzer, and his direct sight and its headrest also are in view to the right of the howitzer.

The turret ring of the 75 mm HMC M8 was larger than that of the Light Tank M5A1, necessitating the elimination of the driver's and assistant driver's hatches in the roof. Instead, both crewmen had a large vision port with an armored door on the glacis. Each of those crewmen also had a front and a side periscope, seen here in the raised position. On the center of the mantlet, the muzzle of the 75 mm howitzer rests inside a larger-diameter sleeve that acted to protect the muzzle.

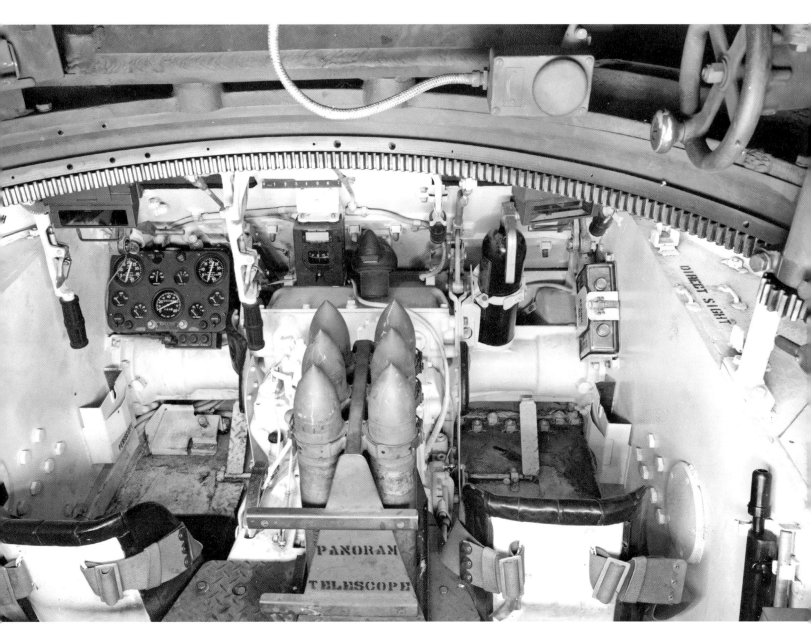

The driver's and assistant driver's compartments of M8 pilot number A1 are viewed from within the turret. There were dual driving controls; the assistant driver's brake and steering levers are stored in clips against the inside of the glacis. Between the seats is a rack for six 75 mm rounds. To the upper right is the handwheel for the traversing gear, which was manually powered only.

In a view of the turret of an M8 from above, on the front right interior are the elevating and traversing handwheels, at right angles to each other. Between those controls and the 75 mm howitzer is the gunner's direct sight. The howitzer breech and recoil cylinders are at the center, and to the left are storage boxes for grenades and .45-caliber ammunition. At the bottom are parts of the .50-caliber machine gun and the ring mount.

The rear half of the M8 turret is viewed from above. In the rear are two M1 carbines, ammunition boxes, a storage bin for binoculars, and a three-gallon oil can. Below the turret in the hull are a fire extinguisher and racks holding 75 mm ammunition in packing tubes.

This photo and the following six show Light Tank M5, serial number 2, registration number 3043436, procured under purchase order T-3159-1 and built by the Cadillac Division in April 1942. This series was taken during evaluations of the vehicle at the Desert Training Center, Indio, California, in June and August 1942. This photo was taken on June 8.

Light Tank M5 number 2 is climbing a rise at the Desert Training Center on June 25, 1942. The tank was rated for climbing a maximum grade of 60 percent and a maximum vertical wall of 18 inches. The fixed .30-caliber machine gun near the center of the glacis, which also was on the M3E3, is present, along with the flexible bow machine gun, but the fixed machine gun would soon be discontinued.

A close inspection of this photograph of Light Tank M5, serial number 2, reveals that the name "QUISENBERRY" is stenciled in small letters on the sponson below the five-gallon liquid container lashed to the turret. A tripod with a dustcover over the machine gun cradle is secured to the right-front fender.

The "QUISENBERRY" inscription was repeated near the center of the left sponson of M5 serial number 2. On the left half of the turret roof are the semicircular guards to the sides of the gunner's periscope. A machine gun tripod with dustcover is strapped to the left fender. On the rear portion of the sponson, note the vertical weld bead to the immediate rear of the radio antenna, and the six roundheaded, slotted screws near the upper edge of the sponson.

The M5 makes a high-speed leap over a sand dune during evaluations at the Desert Training Center on June 25, 1942. It is not clear what the purpose of the arch-shaped fitting on the front right of the glacis was: it was present on the Light Tank M3E3 prototype and the first several M5s.

On the glacis of the Light Tank
M5 below the fixed-bow machine
gun was a crescent-shaped splash
guard, to protect the gun from ricocheting
projectiles. This photo of M5 serial number
2 and registration number 3043436 was
taken at the Desert Training Center in
August 1942. The name "QUISENBERRY"
printed in small block letters is still present
on the sponson. Note the five-gallon
liquid container in a holder on the side
of the turret.

Light Tank M5, serial number 2, is maneuvering along a dusty trail at the Desert Training Center in August 1942. The arrangement of one headlight and one blackout lamp on each side of the glacis and a siren on the inboard side of the left headlight would carry over to later M5s and M5A1s, although the left brush guard later would take on a different shape.

The Light Tank M5's introduction to combat was following the Operation Torch landings in North Africa in November 1942. Here, the crew of an M5 with a prominent US flag on the sponson is on guard duty outside the US-French weather bureau at the Casablanca Airport in French Morocco on November 17, 1942. A crewman is manning the .30-caliber antiaircraft machine gun. A name, which appears to be "ALWAYS," is painted in white to the front of the flag.

Inhabitants of Rabat, French Morocco, are gathered around several Light Tanks M5 during a religious festival on December 19, 1942. A small US flag is painted on the sponson of the closest M5, below the assistant driver's open hatch door. The recognition stars are of a subdued color, not white and likely yellow, and a censor has whited-out unit markings on the final-drive assembly.

A 75 mm Howitzer Motor Carriage M8 is being loaded onto a pontoon raft at an undisclosed location around 1942. Faintly visible is a band of white or light gray around the turret and the mantlet.

In an original World War II color photograph taken at Camp Chorrera, Panama, in March 1943, a Light Tank M5 from the 27th Cavalry is advancing across a field with the driver's and assistant driver's heads above the open hatches. This tank has a variant of the gun shield, or mantlet, with a thick protrusion on the upper part. Different versions of this protrusion are sometimes seen on Stuart light tanks predating the M5s.

In a photograph taken at Camp Chorrera, Panama, on March 11, 1943, seven M5s are lined up during a demonstration by members of the 27th Cavalry. This unit was part of the US forces tasked with the defense of the Panama Canal.

A Light Tank M5 from the 102nd Cavalry has become mired while attempting to negotiate a ravine during a training exercise at Chiseldon Camp, England on March 26, 1943. To the right, another M5 from the 102nd Cavalry has a tow cable attached to the mired tank and is attempting to recover it. A crewman is hanging over the left side of the mired tank, probably to add some weight to that side of the vehicle and increase its traction.

The mired M5 from the 102nd Cavalry is viewed from another perspective while suffering the indignity of becoming mired in a slight ravine at Chiseldon Camp, England, on March 26, 1943. Without grousers installed, the smooth-treaded T16 tracks were quite ineffective on soft ground. Ironically, considering the actual predicament the tank was in, the original Army caption for this photo, titled "All in the Day's Work," boasted that this M5 "disregards all depths of mud, as it saunters over this hill."

Three Light Tanks M5 from the 102nd Cavalry Regiment are lined up, awaiting the order to advance, during maneuvers at Chiseldon Camp, England, on March 26, 1943. The first two tanks have a white graphic of a running bulldog on the sponson to the front of the recognition star; the third tank has a different, indiscernible graphic. Standing in the turret of the nearest tank is Pfc. Calvin Miller, while Sgt. Perry C. Adams is standing in a turret hatch of the third vehicle.

Two crewmen of Company F, Reconnaissance Squadron (Mechanized), 24th Cavalry Regiment, stand by while another crewman cleans the barrel of the 37 mm gun of a Light Tank M5A1 during a firing problem at the Seaford Range, Sussex, England, on March 17, 1943. Although the fourth digit of the registration number is somewhat indistinct, this number appears to be 3047260. If that were the case, this would be an M5A1 completed by Cadillac in March 1943 and rapidly shipped to England for service the same month. The white "TTD" stencil on the side of the turret refers to the Toledo Tank Depot, the site that did the final fitting and preparation for shipment of many Stuart Tanks. The "TTD" stencil is often seen in photos of M5s and M5A1s during this period.

Foot braced against the left mudguard, a crewman evidently is freeing the tow cable from the front-left tow shackle on a Light Tank M5A1 that has become bogged in thick, soupy mud during a training exercise at the Santa Anita Ordnance School, Santa Anita, California, in April 1943. The .30-caliber machine guns for the bow and coaxial mounts are not installed.

Knapsacks and bedrolls are arrayed on the front of a dust-caked Light Tank M5 on a road march near Maknassy (in Arabic, *Al Miknāsī*), Tunisia, on April 8, 1943. Coming up behind the Stuart are a Jeep and an M3A1 Scout Car.

An M5A1 is parked in an equipment yard at Mediterranean Base Section Ordnance, Oran, Algeria, on April 6, 1943. Various stencils and chalk markings are on the vehicle, signifying that certain tasks have been performed to ready the vehicle for service. These include "Radio OK" (written two times), "Road Test OK," "Small Arms OK," "Lube OK," and "Automotive OK." There is also a chalked notice that the vehicle was "2 Tow Links short."

A US Marine Corps Light Tank M5A1 is engaged in a training exercise in Australia on July 10, 1943. The turret bustle, which was a unique characteristic of the M5A1, is clearly visible, as is the right hatch-door stop, another distinctive feature of the M5A1.

Maj. Gen. William H. Rupertus, commanding general of the 1st Marine Division, *left*, and Lt. Col. Charles G. Meints, commander of the 1st Marine Tank Battalion, confer with each other while inspecting M5A1s from the 1st Marine Tank Battalion at a base in Australia on July 10, 1943. Grousers have been installed at intervals on the tanks' tracks for added traction on the soft ground.

Crewmen of the 1st Marine Tank Battalion pause for their photograph during a training exercise at Balcombe Camp, Australia, on July 10, 1943. The grousers on this vehicle were attached to the tracks at varying intervals, some having seven track links between them and others as few as three or four links. About a foot below the top of the glacis, to the front of the driver's and the assistant driver's stations, was a peephole with a removable, round plug and a U-shaped splash guard.

Brothers and sergeants Walter and John Scott, in the turret of an M5A1 nicknamed "KATIE DID," receive a newspaper from Capt. Richard F. Thomas, from the Scotts' hometown, during a lull in the action in the Capua sector of Italy in November 1945. All three soldiers were members of the 13th Armored Regiment, 1st Armored Division, 5th Army. The tank was camouflaged with an overspray of Earth Yellow paint over Olive Drab. Note the faint outline of a recognition star enclosed in a circle next to the "KATIE DID" marking.

Stuart light tanks, including an M5 in the foreground, from the 27th Cavalry are lined up during a demonstration at Camp Chorrera, Panama, on November 3, 1943.

A Light Tank M5A1 from the 4th Marine Tank Battalion is advancing off the beachhead during the invasion of Namur Island, Kwajalein Atoll, on February 1, 1944. The tank's nickname, "HOTHEAD," is painted in a dark color on the forward end of the sponson. Light-colored swatches of camouflage paint have been applied over the base color. Faintly visible to the rear of the "HOTHEAD" marking is a stenciled half circle, the symbol of the 4th Marine Division. *Jim Gilmore collection*

At a training area outside Prato, Italy, an M5A1 from the 1st Armored Division is about to be towed out of a ravine, where it became mired while attempting to cross a fascine made of tree trunks lashed around a steel culvert.

At an unidentified training site in the desert, tank crewmen are practice-firing the antiaircraft machine guns mounted on the sides of the turrets. The first three tanks are M5A1s, with .30-caliber machine guns mounted on the right sides of the turrets. Farther along are five Medium Tanks M4, with .50-caliber machine guns. The nickname "DORIS" is painted on the sponson of the second M5A1.

An M5A1 from the 1st Armored Division is operating among the ruins of Cisterna, Italy, on May 25, 1944. A darker camouflage paint has been applied in swatches over the Olive Drab base color of the tank, and a rack, probably made of a wooden plank, has been placed between the front fenders to hold stowed equipment on the glacis. A five-gallon liquid container is in a rack on the right fender.

On June 4, 1944, a 1st Armored Division M5A1 is picking its way through a debris-clogged street during the advance to Rome. Two logs, always useful for various scenarios, have been attached to the left side of the hull with wire. A Periscope M6 is protruding above the commander's hatch door, and identical periscopes are on the driver's and assistant driver's hatch doors.

On Route 7 outside Rome on June 4, 1944, the date that city fell to the Allies, flames and smoke are issuing from the engine deck of a knocked-out Light Tank M5A1 from the 1st Armored Division, while M8 Greyhound armored cars approach. Visible, serious damage has been done to the right fender and suspension, and the right track is missing.

During the invasion of Saipan in June–July 1944, the crewmen of a 75 mm HMC M8 pause for their photograph during a lull in combat. Markings on the front of the hull are "T" and "CN" followed by an illegible number. Between the driver's and assistant driver's hatches is a painted design of unclear meaning. An extra machine gun, of .30 caliber, has been mounted on the left front of the turret and is fed from the ammo box on the roof of the hull next to the turret. On the inboard side of that gun is a periscope head.

Just after D-day, June 6, 1944, a Stuart VI, based on the Light Tank M5A1, is leading a column of Stuarts along a dusty road in Normandy. As was usual with British tanks, additional ammunition boxes have been emplaced on the vehicle; these are visible on the fenders and the glacis. Also, smoke-grenade launchers have been mounted: two of them are on the outboard side of the machine gun shield on the right side of the turret.

The four members of the crew of a Light Tank M5A1 from the 762nd Tank Battalion, 27th Infantry Division, are taking a brief respite during the invasion of Saipan in early July 1944. All four men are identified. *Left to right*, they are Pvt. John Coakley, assistant driver; Lt. James A. Bulloch, vehicle commander; Pfc. Louis Tocci, gunner; and Tech. 4 Jesús Tijerina, driver.

American tanks encountered a seemingly insurmountable obstacle during fighting in the hedgerows of Normandy in the summer of 1944. These dense hedgerows, often atop embankments surrounding fields, were difficult if not impossible for tanks to punch through. Enter Sgt. Curtis G. Culin III, from the 102nd Cavalry Reconnaissance Squadron, who designed a plow-like device, fashioned from scrap structural steel (often from German-fabricated obstacles) and attached to the bows of tanks. This device, dubbed the Culin hedgerow cutter, allowed tanks, such as the M5A1 shown here, to readily force their way through hedgerows, thus denying the Germans a key defensive aid they had enjoyed. Sandbags have been piled on the glacis for additional protection.

Sgt. Curtis Culin, inventor of the Culin hedgerow cutter, is standing in the driver's hatch of a Light Tank M5A1 in France on July 30, 1944. The original label of the photo mentions that the Culin device also was referred to as the "Rhino."

On a vehicle-jammed street near Saint-Fromond, France, on July 11, 1944, is a Light Tank M5A1 in the foreground. It is registration number 3051254, completed in May 1943 by the Southern California Division of GM. On the sponson are the code "C-34" and the nickname "CAROL." Markings on the bow are for Company C, 33rd Armored Regiment, 3rd Armored Division. Another M5A1 is to the rear of the Jeep in the foreground. *Jim Gilmore collection*

Another M5A1 from Company C, 33rd Armored Regiment, this one coded "C-14" on the sponson, is moving through a narrow street corner in the vicinity of Saint-Fromond, France, on July 11, 1944. This Stuart bears the nickname "CISCO KID" on the sponson: the letter *C* in the C-14 code partially obscures the word "KID." Shipping data is stenciled in white on the front end of the sponson.

A military policeman observes as a Massey-Harris Light Tank M5A1, registration number 3065475, completed in April 1943, advances through Saint-Paul-de-Vernay, Normandy, on July 17, 1944. Baggage and equipment are piled high on the rear of the engine deck. The nickname "CONCRETE" is stenciled in white on the forward end of the sponson.

During the pursuit of the rapidly retreating German forces in France on July 27, 1944, a Light Tank M5A1 nicknamed "WASP" is passing a Jeep in a destroyed village. A large, white recognition star inside a white circle is painted on the turret roof.

A Light Tank M5A1 with a Culin hedgerow cutter laden with clods of dirt advances through a field in Normandy on July 21, 1944. The registration number on the sponson appears to be 30480195: if so, this was a vehicle completed by Cadillac in September 1943. Next to the shipping data stencil on the sponson is the nickname "DEAR RUTHIE."

As if to punctuate the warning sign concerning buried land mines, an M5A1 that has had its right suspension destroyed by a mine lies in a road in Coutances, France, on July 30, 1944. A spare idler wheel was stored on the glacis.

Crewmen are performing maintenance in the field on a 75 mm Howitzer Motor Carriage M8, registration number 4052227, during a lull in combat outside Barenton, France, on August 9, 1944. The crewman standing on the Culin hedgerow cutter is preparing to clean the barrel of the 75 mm howitzer. A large pile of 75 mm rounds are on the ground; to the right are the fiberboard packing tubes the rounds were stored in until they were ready, or almost ready, to be fired. The vehicle nickname "LAXATIVE" and the code "3-9" are painted on the sponson.

A disabled Light Tank M5A1 with the left track missing is being winched onto an M19 tank transporter, consisting of an M9 trailer hitched to a Diamond T M20 truck-tractor. The left track has been rolled up and stored on the turret, secured with a chain. "Sandbag armor" had been arranged on the glacis, to improve the tank's chances of surviving a frontal antitank projectile hit.

An American infantryman scurries across a road while a Light Tank M5A1 provides fire support during an effort to knock out a German machine gun nest along a road near Coudray, France, on August 8, 1944.

Three destroyed M5A1s are lying in the salvage yard of the 821st Heavy Maintenance Company at Grossoto, Italy, on September 1, 1944. The bow of the tank to the left has been blown off, exposing the differential, final drive, and detached instrument panel inside. The two other tanks have markings on the bows for Company B, 13th Armored Regiment, 1st Armored Division.

Several M5A1s from the 4th Armored Division, including one with sandbag armor and a Culin hedgerow cutter in the foreground, are passing through newly liberated Saint-Armand, France, on September 2, 1944. On the lead tank, the bow machine gun has been dismounted, and a section of spare track is stored on the bottom of the glacis.

Geese peck for food near an M5A1 that has been emplaced in a static-defense position in the no-man's
land near the Siegfried Line, outside Baesweiler, in the Aachen sector of Germany, on October 19, 1944.
The vehicle commander is standing up in the turret, surveying the terrain for threats.

Three M5A1s from the 13th Tank Battalion are on the advance outside Bambiano, Italy, in October 1944. The tank in the center has the nickname "Paper Doll" painted, within quotation marks, on the sponson, and another name, "BABS," is painted on the side of the turret. All three tanks have white bands painted on the 37 mm gun barrels and are painted in camouflage, with at least one lighter color applied over the standard Olive Drab.

A woman leading a cow is the subject of scrutiny by the crew of a Light Tank M5A1 halted on a road through war-ravaged Beauzemont, France, in October 1944. The driver's windshield is mounted on its bracket on the upper left of the glacis, and a Culin hedgerow cutter is installed on the bow.

Infantrymen from Company B, 1st Battalion, 114th Infantry Regiment, 44th Division, mount M5A1s preparatory to an attack on Struth, in the Lohr sector of France, on November 28, 1944. On close inspection of the photo, the glacis of the nearest M5A1 appears to be covered with sand and the remnants of shot-up textile from sandbags. Several intact sandbags are visible above the retainer pipe running across the bow.

A 75 mm Howitzer Mortar Carrier M8, registration number 4052231, is boarding an M25 tank transporter at a site in France in late November 1944. Another M8 is already loaded on the transporter trailer, and to the rear is another, partially visible M8, registration number 4052495, with the name "Lily 'X'?" painted on the sponson.

This M5A1 from the 4th Armored Division is performing duty as a battle ambulance, as crewmen lift a patient on a stretcher from the engine deck of the tank, at an aid station during the fighting along the Saar River, on December 1, 1944. Tanks were being used as ambulances at this time because of the heavy casualties from enemy artillery fire and the muddy conditions of the roads.

Three M5A1s from the 709th Tank Battalion, 9th Infantry Division, V Corps, have taken up a position along the ruins of a building on the German frontier on December 24, 1944. The tank in the center has a Culin hedgerow cutter and racks made of steel rods on both sponsons. The tank to the right has the bottom section of a deep-fording trunk on the rear of the hull.

On December 27, 1944, M5A1s from Company D, 37th Tank Battalion, 4th Armored Division, are escorting a column of trucks, part of a force preparing to relieve US forces surrounded by the Germans in Bastogne, Belgium.

An M5A1 from Troop B, 106th Cavalry Reconnaissance Squadron, 106th Cavalry Group, XV Corps, has just fired a 37 mm high-explosive round at a house occupied by German troops along the German frontier on December 29, 1944. Stowage racks made of angle iron have been welded to the rear corners of the upper hull and a deep-fording trunk, and the numeral "2" has been painted roughly on the sponson.

In a humanitarian act, members of the crew of an M5A1 from the 37th Armored Regiment, 3rd Armored Division, are bringing a wounded German soldier, huddled under a blanket on the glacis, to an aid station in Echtz, Germany, in late December 1944. A dead German soldier is lying along the road in the foreground. The head of the wounded German is visible above the driver's head, which is elevated above his hatch; the German's right boot is next to the left headlight.

Two GIs survey the damage caused when a German plane bombed this courtyard in Betschdorf, France, on January 10, 1945. The bomb detonated five boxes of land mines stored there, severely damaging the M5A1 parked there. The left sprocket and final drive were torn off, and much general damage was done to the tank.

M5A1 registration number 3089898, with the nickname "SHANTY IRISH" painted at the front of the sponson, has taken position in the town square of Rouffach, France, on February 5, 1945. This is a late-production M5A1, with the storage box and a tow pintle on the rear of the hull.

Next to the large pile of 75 mm ammunition-packing tubes in the foreground, a 75 mm HMC M8 from the 106th Cavalry Reconnaissance Group is shelling enemy forces near Geslautern, Germany, on February 8, 1945. An ammunition trailer is parked to the rear of the M8, and another large pile of ammo-packing tubes is in the right background.

African American trainees are manning a Light Tank M5A1, numbered "68" on the glacis, at the Armored School Detachment, Replacement and Training Command, near Naples, Italy, on March 1, 1945. In the commander's hatch is Pfc. Dewey McClain; in the assistant driver's hatch is Pvt. Hulett McHenry, while the driver is Pfc. Lester Baker.

A crewman of an M5A1 with Company D, 34th Tank Battalion, is manning the .30-caliber antiaircraft machine gun on a street in Viersen, Germany, on March 3, 1945. On the glacis next to the box on the right fender are a half loaf of bread on a stack of two tin plates, and a pair of arctic overshoes with rubber bottoms and waterproof canvas tops.

An M5A1 from the 3rd Armored Division is passing by a burning building during the advance through Ludwigshutte, Germany, on March 29, 1945. Two five-gallon liquid containers and a tarpaulin-covered box are stored on the glacis of the tank. The crew and riders all are wearing M1 steel helmets, which was customary when operating out of the confines of the tank in nonsecure areas.

On April 10, 1945, less than one month before the official surrender of Germany, a Light Tank M5A1 from the 5th Armored Division, Ninth Army, is driving through Peine, Germany. On the front of the turret roof is a large loudspeaker, through which a message was being broadcast to any remaining German forces to surrender.

Parked among other tanks in an assembly area of the 12th Armored Division outside Nassig, Germany, in early April 1945, are two late-production M5A1s with the armored shields for the antiaircraft machine guns. However, new mounts for these machine guns have been attached to the right sides of the turrets to the front of the machine gun shields, apparently to allow the vehicle commander to more easily fire the gun to the front. The tank on the left was equipped with mudguards, left over from the original sand skirt set, which are badly battered. That tank has T16 tracks, while the one to the right has the T36E6 tracks. *Jim Gilmore collection*

An M5A1 is accompanying dismounted cavalry troops from Company F, Troop B, 116th Cavalry Reconnaissance Squadron (Mechanized), Seventh Army, through the town of Weilheim, Bavaria, in late April 1945. The tank has sandbag armor on the glacis, held in place by a beam between the fenders. The large recognition star on the sponson is cut off at the bottom; the lower part of the star originally was painted on sand skirts, which have been removed.

An M5A1 from the 91st Reconnaissance Squadron, 1st Armored Division, is crossing a pontoon bridge over the Po River in the San Benedetto area of Italy on April 25, 1945. Two five-gallon liquid containers are stored on the glacis, supported in part by the splash guard. In the background, another M5A1 is driving down the draw toward the bridge.

Sgt. Walter W. Burega, of Company D, 751st Tank Battalion, gives a tutorial on his M5A1 to members of the Swiss border guards on the Swiss-Italian border on May 6, 1945. The unit marking for the 751st Tank Battalion is on the upper part of the glacis. In addition to the metal boxes stored on the front of the tank, there is a German gas mask canister.

Elements of the 784th Tank Battalion, an African American unit in the wartime, racially segregated US Army, have paused in a German hamlet on May 5, 1945, two days before the German surrender. In addition to the Jeep alongside the road and the half-track backed into the garage, there are five Light Tanks M5 parked along the road. The crewman on the M5A1 to the far right is handing 37 mm ammunition into the turret. *Jim Gilmore collection*

Some tank-destroyer battalions employed Light Tanks M5A1 for scouting purposes. Such was the case with this M5A1 from the 705th Tank Destroyer Battalion, 11th Armored Division, US Third Army, ceremoniously driving over a long Nazi banner in Lembach, Germany, on May 4, 1945. An extra .30-caliber machine gun has been mounted on the turret. Crew names are painted on the short splash guards on the glacis: on the right-hand splash guard is one for a Sgt. Coulter. "PRESTONE 44" stenciled on the top center of the glacis indicates that antifreeze was added to the coolant during 1944. The object on the center of the glacis appears to have been a spindle for storing a spare bogie wheel.

The crews of two Light Tanks M5A1 armed with Model E7-7 flamethrowers in the turrets, assigned to the 13th Armored Group, pose in their vehicles on Luzon, Philippines, on August 3, 1945. These were two of four M5A1 flamethrower light tanks that arrived on Luzon four months earlier, on April 3, 1945. The vehicles were in the combat zone for service testing, and they were equipped with one maintenance truck.

By the end of World War II, the Light Tanks M5 and M5A1 and the 75 mm Howitzer Motor Carriage M8 were obsolete and were rapidly being supplanted by more-modern and better-armed vehicles. Many of these vehicles were placed in storage or transferred to America's allies. A multitude of other vehicles, particularly in the more remote areas of the Pacific, were simply abandoned or turned into scrap. In this photo, 75 mm HMC M8 vehicles are on a dock at Manila, Philippines, awaiting disposal in March 1946.